An UNEXPECTED SHOW and TELL

By Jessiey James

Illustrations by Carolyn Mottern

To order additional copies of this book, contact:
Xlibris
844-714-8691
www.Xlibris.com
Orders@Xlibris.com

ISBN: Softcover   978-1-6641-7058-2
       Hardcover   978-1-6641-7056-8
       EBook   978-1-6641-7057-5

Print information available on the last page

Rev. date: 04/26/2021

DEDICATION

To my children: Brandon, Jarrett and Jenna

Everything happens when I am at Preschool. Today, my mom, Jessie, and DeAnna, our housekeeper, were outside in front of our house. As DeAnna was getting in her car, she looked down and saw a turtle.

The turtle was on its way to the street. DeAnna immediately picked it up and handed it to my mom.

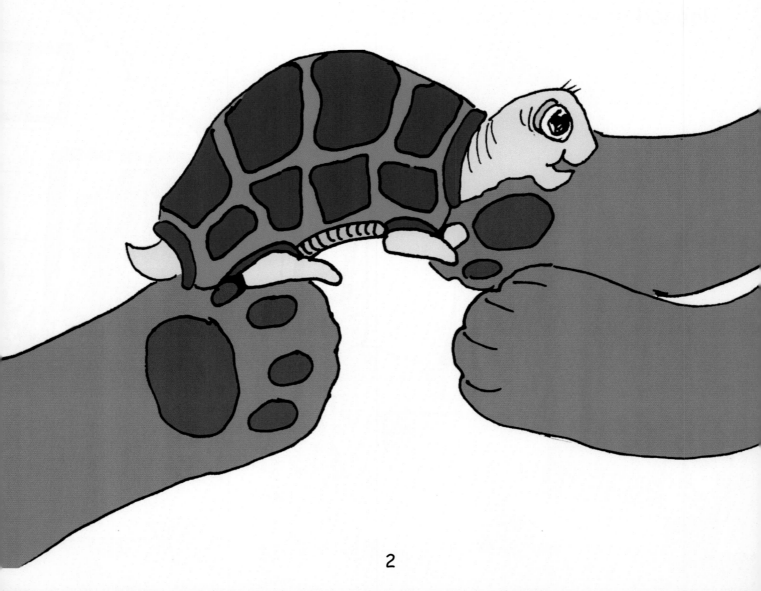

My mom was trying to find our cat, Gordon. I am to bring Gordon to school for Show and Tell. My mom cannot find Gordon. He must be hiding. Unable to find Gordon, my mom suddenly decides to bring the turtle. My mom puts the turtle in a small white bucket. She drives to my school.

My Preschool is downstairs in a big Church. My Teacher is Mrs. Eaves. She always has a big smile when I and the other kids come. We have another teacher. Her name is Miss Robins. She is very pretty.

I am so excited when my mom walks in with my Show and Tell. I ask: "Is Gordon in the bucket"? She shakes her head. She points inside the bucket. I look. I'm not sure what it is. It is green and yellow. I ask: "What is it"? My mom replies: "It's a turtle". I have never seen a real turtle.

Jennie Lynn

5

The other kids in my class gather around the bucket to take a peek inside. We take turns holding the turtle, but very carefully.

A boy in my class, Matt, puts the turtle on the carpet. Surprisingly, it crawls. Matt yells:

"Way to go Freddie"!

It's time to go. My mom and I take the turtle to our car. My mom lets me put the white bucket with the turtle in the backseat. That is where I ride.

We are going to pick up my brothers at another school I call the "The Big School". They are in 2nd and 4th Grade. I remark: "Wait till Brandyn and Jared see the turtle." My mom says:

"Let's try and keep this a surprise".

PAW PRINT ELEMENTARY

9

First, Brandyn gets in the car. Immediately he starts telling us what happened in Gym class. His class was playing golf. A boy in his class, Joshua, got mad and threw a golf club at a golf bag. The club ended up in the bag. Brandyn said the whole class cheered. But his Teacher gave Joshua a bad behavior check for throwing the club.

10

Brandyn doesn't notice the bucket lying on the floor in the back seat. When my other brother, Jared gets in the car, he stops. He remarks: "What do we have here?"

Jared asks: "Whose turtle?" I say: "I don't know. A boy in my class called him Freddie". Jared says: "Will we be able to keep it?" I say: "I don't know".

As soon as we get home, my brothers and I are anxious to show the neighbor kids the turtle. Several kids gather around the white bucket.

Andrea, our next door neighbor, says she saw a poster on the telephone pole about a reward for a lost turtle. We all run over to the telephone pole. There is a yellow paper thumb tacked to the pole. Brandyn reads:

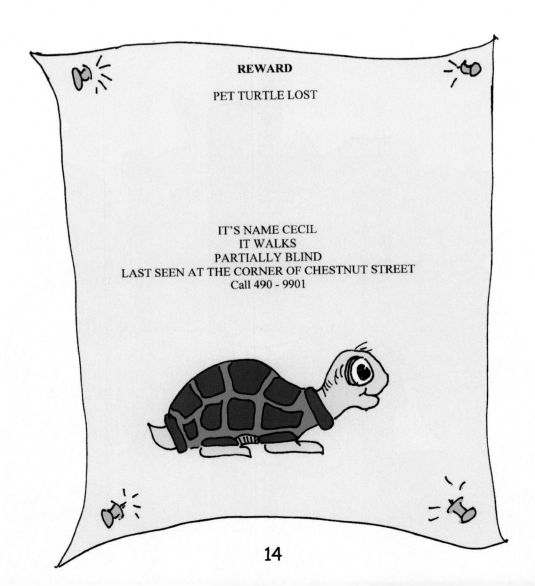

REWARD

PET TURTLE LOST

IT'S NAME CECIL
IT WALKS
PARTIALLY BLIND
LAST SEEN AT THE CORNER OF CHESTNUT STREET
Call 490 - 9901

After my brothers finish their homework, my mother calls the number on the yellow paper. We need to take the turtle to Luke McDaniel that lives at 2932 Chestnut Street.

I, my brothers, Brandyn and Jared, Andrea, our neighbor, and my mom are going to walk over to the McDaniel's house. Andrea picks up the bucket with the turtle.

We walk to the McDaniel's house. Brandyn rings the doorbell. We introduce ourselves to Mrs. McDaniel and Luke McDaniel.

Andrea hands Luke the bucket with the turtle. The McDaniel's thank us for returning the turtle.

Mrs. McDaniel then gives me, my brothers and Andrea each a five dollar bill. She says:

"This is your reward."

Luke McDowell runs over to an aquarium. When he returns, he has a turtle smaller than Cecil in a plastic bowl.

Mrs. McDaniel says: "Jessie, would you allow these children to have this turtle since Cecil is already Luke's pet?" My mom nods. I jump up and down. Mrs. McDaniel asks:

"Would you like to take home this turtle?" We all reply: "YES."

Luke walks over to the aquarium again. He opens a cupboard door on the bottom and runs back. Luke says: "Here is some food for this turtle until you can get some at the store." Andrea says: "Thank you."

As we are walking home, Andrea remarks: "I think Luke has more turtles. I plan to ask my parents if I am allowed to get one."

Meanwhile, Jared and I are trying to come up with a name for this turtle. I wonder what shall we call him? What if he is a girl?

Printed in the United States
by Baker & Taylor Publisher Services